YOUR KNOWLEDGE HA

- We will publish your bachelor's and master's thesis, essays and papers

- Your own eBook and book - sold worldwide in all relevant shops

- Earn money with each sale

Upload your text at www.GRIN.com
and publish for free

Bibliographic information published by the German National Library:

The German National Library lists this publication in the National Bibliography; detailed bibliographic data are available on the Internet at http://dnb.dnb.de .

Imprint:

Copyright © 2013 GRIN Verlag, Open Publishing GmbH
Print and binding: Books on Demand GmbH, Norderstedt Germany
ISBN: 9783668372382

This book at GRIN:

http://www.grin.com/en/e-book/349951/danish-cartoons-and-freedom-of-speech-principles-of-harm-and-offence

Ghazanfar Ahmad Adnan

Danish Cartoons and Freedom of Speech. Principles of Harm and Offence

GRIN Publishing

GRIN - Your knowledge has value

Since its foundation in 1998, GRIN has specialized in publishing academic texts by students, college teachers and other academics as e-book and printed book. The website www.grin.com is an ideal platform for presenting term papers, final papers, scientific essays, dissertations and specialist books.

Visit us on the internet:

http://www.grin.com/

http://www.facebook.com/grincom

http://www.twitter.com/grin_com

Human Rights II

Module IV B-Thesis Malmo University

DANISH CARTOONS AND FREEDOM OF SPEECH

Ghazanfar Ahmad Adnan

Abstract

The problem emerges as a result of cartoons of Prophet Mohammad (P.B.U.H.) in 2005 by the Danish Newspaper "Jayllands Posten". It created a situation that exposed the differences of different worlds based on religions and beliefs. Freedom of expression and opinion in international instruments based on acknowledged human rights became controversial in relation to rights and duties. In regards to Danish cartoons, principles of harm and offence as explained by Mill and Feinberg and their legal validity are applied to judge the situation. Laws are based on norms and values philosophically exerted out of customs and practices. I would present that human behaviors are meant to be treated based on realities but not on cynic philosophical argumentations or debates.

DANISH CARTOONS AND FREEDOM OF SPEECH

Table of contents

DANISH CARTOONS AND FREEDOM OF SPEECH

Chapter 1

1.1 Introduction

Freedom of expression and speech is a right of each and every person to deliver his thoughts through whatever medium he likes, which includes receiving and seeking information and ideas. Everyday progress of life has proved globalization a reality and all its emerging challenges need to be solved and resolved in peace and through mutual understanding of each other. Differences between peoples, nations, communities, religions, and cultures are associated to our beliefs; whether they are conflicts or contrasts between above mentioned groups. Moral norms and values are the deciding platforms to resolve conflicts peacefully. Laws are made and created on norms and values and human progress is in progressive evolution to create new laws each and every day through better understanding of these norms and values. Freedom of speech and expression is one of the rights needs to be understood at every level of human contact and a rational decision is required to resolve the conflict between both opponents. It is a recognised fact that laws are not certain or absolute at any level of human knowledge and their ability depends upon progressive understanding of norms and values regarding human rights as prescribed by human rights scholars and professors. Rona K.M Smith understands this phenomenon and delineates;

> "The breath of articles inevitably is conducive to teleological interpretation in keeping with the progressive evolution of the rights. As society advances, more rights are realized and moral and global standards change. Human rights are not static: they are inherently flexible; the precise meaning of rights may change over the years."[1]

Life is dynamic, and so as the man and society. Social values emerged out of plural and mixed societies, are based on difference and dispute. Difference or the right to differ is the root to knowledge and progress. We should try our level best to safeguard the right to differ in a way that our differences in every field of life that includes religion, philosophy, science, social, economic, political or whatever, should be beneficial and not destructive. When these differences

---

1 Smith, Rona ed.4 Textbook on International Human Rights. 2010. Oxford University Press, USA

become destructive they are to be regulated and resolved through peaceful process and that is only possible if we all submit voluntarily, and if needed reluctantly to the law.

Danish cartoons violence was initiated in response to a complaint by a Danish author of children's book about the life of Muhammad (P.B.U.H.), "Kare Bluitgen" that he could not find any author brave enough to illustrate his book.[2] In 2005, a Danish newspaper, Jayllands Posten published cartoons containing satirical depiction of Prophet Muhammad (P.B.U.H.). Islamic world protested with anger and distress on grounds that Muslim belief doesn't accept any kind of pictorial representation of the Prophet Muhammad (P.B.U.H.). Cartoons associated Prophet and Muslims with terrorism[3]. After the publication of the book which caused some reaction "but its publication was over shadowed the next phase of the affair".[4] Editor of Jayllands Posten invited cartoonists to draw cartoons of Prophet Muhammad (P.B.U.H.)[5], and initial reaction was only peaceful reaction involving 3500 protestors in Copenhagen.[6] On 19th October 2005, a group of Muslim Ambassadors requested a meeting with Danish minister to discuss the cartoons, which was refused.[7] Six people were killed in attack on Danish Embassy in Pakistan in June 2008,.[8] Staff from embassies in Afghanistan and Algeria were evacuated in April 2008 following to terror threat linked to reprinting of cartoons.[9] According to an estimate this issue has taken 139 lives.[10] This was taken as a lawful act within the framework of the right of freedom of expression throughout the West.

1.2 Aims of Research

My purpose of research on the cartoons violence issue is to explain the moral grounds of universal human rights standards required to solve the dilemma peacefully. I have presented past, present and future of the controversy. All the conflict is misrepresented if they are presented out of context in relation to discussing the history of the conflict. For instance all the conflicts which

2, 10 Post, Robert(2007), Religion and freedom of speech: Portraits of Muhammad, Constellation Volume 14, No1,72-90

3 Sturges, Paul (2006), Limits to freedom of expression? Considerations arising from the Danish cartoon affair.IFLA Journal 32(3) 181-188

4-9 Keane, David (2008), Cartoon Violence and freedom of Expression. Human Rights Quarterly 30 845-875

are a threat to world peace have long history. And almost all the conflicts are based on religious grounds, for instance Palestine, Kashmir and the recent phenomenon terrorism is not out of this circle at all. My aim was to understand and give a brief but broad view of the cartoon controversy by describing its past as well. Describing religious conflict as the historical background does not mean we are still following the past but my aim was to show the current situation of our world which has become a global village in which personal bias of a single person can escalate a world conflict if few people decide to manipulate the situation. I certainly disprove any "clash of civilizations" but wanted to explain how we can build bridges among different cultural and social differences.

1.3 Research Questions

1- How can we understand the cartoon controversy in historical perspective?

2- What does legal international law posses to limit freedom of speech?

3-Can we limit fee speech on philosophical and moral grounds?

1.4 Theory

I used a combination of legal and philosophical theories to explain, what are the legal responsibilities to preserve one's right against other and what are philosophically defined terms and norm exist to safeguard rights against violator if proved as violations. I used Mill and Feinburg for their harm and offence principle theories in relation to limiting freedom of speech and applied them on the case of my thesis to identify whether philosophy provides moral grounds to limit free speech in certain situations or not.

1.5 Method and Material

I used the combination of legal method with the argumentation analysis for my research is more based on all forms of legal documents including domestic, regional and international legal systems analysis. Laws are exerted through norms and values in to legal form and their relation is fundamentally joined together as both equally complement each other. My first part is related to legal analysis and the other part is the norm and value analysis of freedom of speech. Legal method of research is the best suited research method for my paper as my research is about laws based on norms and how laws can be limited by other conflicting laws and how norms shape existing laws. How norms can even generate new laws Shelton describes legal method; "....choice of law between conflicting norms of equivalent status, although one obvious means of resolving a conflict is to designate one norm or subject matter as hierarchically superior to others."[11]

I am using argumentation analysis because there are very specific occurrences of arguments and counter arguments about how laws can be limited by replacing them with other superior laws or what norms are more reliable and what should be compromised for other norms. I have presented how reasons causes different controversies which is a relater to arguments to show the complete ifs and buts as in the case of argumentation analysis Weston delineates, "Here we come to arguments about cause and their effects—about what causes what. Such arguments are often vital." [12]

We found that it would be far more interesting to state the exact violations of rights if we found any. For this to be possible, we are going to be looking at several human rights documents such as the International Convention on Civil and Political Rights, the Universal Declaration of the Human Rights, the Declaration on the Elimination of All Forms of Intolerance and of Discrimination Based on Religion or Belief, the Declaration on the Rights of Persons Belonging to National or Ethnic, Religious or Linguistic Minorities and regional documents of equal status. To deal with the part related to norms and values, mainly I used Mill's harm principle, and Feinburge's offence principle, for these two are highly regarded philosophers in relation to free speech. Furthermore, Stanley Fish and David Mill were explained to compliment harm and offence principles.

11 Shelton, Dinah. (2006) Normative Hierarchy in International Law Author(s) The American Journal of International Law, Vol. 100, No. 2 pp. 29

12 Weston, Anthony. A Rulebook for Arguments. 2009. Hackett Publishing Company Inc. USA

1.6 Disposition

In chapter2, I have given a historical perspective of my topic freedom of speech in relation to cartoons controversy. This chapter is about the religious conflicts that existed since long, and how in present still can be escalated even by a biased individual can turn these in to violent clash. Chapter3 is about legal issues through which freedom of speech can be limited if it is required. Chapter4 is related to norms and values which can become an instrument to limit the extended free speech.

Chapter 2

2.1 Historical Background into Religious Hatred and Cartoons Controversy

It is very important to realistically present some historical facts which are the core of the conflict unresolved, and are a natural phenomenon of not being able to understand and resolve the real problem. There is a long history of defaming religion and its purposes and persons. Whether it is Judaism, Christianity, Islam or any religion, it had always been under criticism by the nonbelievers or opponents of each other. Laws were put into actions based on purely so called religious jurisprudence as state laws, like blasphemy laws. Although under these laws people were brutally killed in past, and we have the worst examples ever existed of human disorder and anarchy. The playground of religious brutality continued for centuries. In the name of blasphemy, whenever one got dominance and their opponent became minority, like Jews persecuted Christians being blasphemous towards their beliefs in the very first centuries of Christianity. When Christians were in majority against Jews they did the same to their opponents, the Jews. These brutalities sometimes turned into a religion as contradictions in beliefs within one religion become inevitable as in the case of Catholics and Protestants, and in Islam, Shea and Sunni brutal conflicts can be experienced to this day even.

Sometimes these conflicts turned between religion and modern non religious believes such as science. Copernicus theory is one example of such conflicts between religion and science. Such clashes resulted in burning of scientists. Galileo had to deny a natural fact which was seen as blasphemy to the religion if his theory, earth not being flat and moving around the sun, is to be considered. As a result of such stupid practises, Christian world had to get rid of such unrealistic ideas of religion and that resistance against religion turned into a reaction and the religions were left altogether not having any contribution in state affairs. Blasphemy laws to safeguard religions were not seen as important and useful because of their historical reputation. West did not have a problem of religious minorities being marginalized or persecuted by other religious majorities for religions do not have any power over secular governments. Now the conflicts between religions or sects of a religion turned into conflict between nonreligious secular governments and religions. Blasphemy laws were not important anymore and if the religion was criticised, it was not taken seriously by the people because of the long association and bloody history of these conflicts. Masses did not react strongly what they could have done centuries back.

In the recent century, globalization made the world changed in its every aspect including society and state affairs because of the migrant societies, cultures, traditions, and religions. Islam is the second largest religion of Europe, and a reality. The culture and traditions Islam had, travelled with Muslims and the conflict between religion and secularism emerged in a new form for now Europe was not related to only one religion anymore and the religious evolution through the course of history was not similar in Europe. Although the criticism against religion in the media was not new but in the case of Islam, it was against a religion which was not related to Europe as a part of its history and it created the controversies between religion and secular ideals. Islam as the youngest religion among monotheistic religions is going through the dilapidated evolutionary process which Christianity had experienced centuries back in which religious forces are fundamentally rigid and uncompromising against all opponents. All the Islamic sects are turned violent among each other and against the non Muslim beliefs. This is a situation in which opportunists can very easily manipulate religious association of masses into violent beliefs and it can cause serious threats to peace and stability in the world. These differences are needed to be taken seriously by both religious and non religious counterparts. Islam became a controversial topic and historians explained it out of context and history, hence made it controversial and complicated to understand the history of relation of Islam and Christianity into the relation between Islam and West. Many opportunists took it for granted to propagate their nationalist political agenda as in the case of Danish Cartoons, Danish Political party tried to mix things up and made it difficult to control the situation for the government as a spokesperson of the Danish Peoples Party, Soren Kararup, said that; "Muslims Immigration is a way for Muslims to conquer us, just as the way they have done 1400 years past." [13]

This phenomenon has to be judged and looked into very precisely and with complete awareness of later mistakes which were done by the people with hidden agendas to keep differences and hatred alive between nations and communities in the name of religion and fundamentally nationalist theories to gain their popularity in masses so that they could get majority or somewhat representation at the highest levels of authority over humanity. It is very easy way to get popularity in masses to manipulate their association with their beliefs through playing game of hatred. Such examples used to exist in past to divide humanity and in the name of religion and belief which are still lurking in air to use them as an old weapon. New era has gained such an enlightened and rational awareness of understanding and importance of reason that we know if there exist anything superior and better to improve our relations and situations then it must be adopted against an inferior ideology or belief. With broader visions and understanding of past through research we are able to understand and make people understand the situation which scholars revealed as mysteries what used to become purpose of differences and conflicts. In past, defaming your opponent was a basic rule to have strong shekels over majorities in the name of religion and nationalism.

Karen Armstrong is one of the scholars who have deep knowledge of religions and have written books about history of religious evolution. She has a deep knowledge of religious texts and the course of their conflicts and strategies they used to keep hold of certain majorities by defaming other religions as she reveals the pattern of western religious scholars how they kept hatred alive for Islam and hence created an air of distance between east and west in the name of religion. She writes; "..Islam as being one major religion which 'seems to be outside this circle of goodwill and, in West at least, to have retained its negative image...even though it is the third religion of Abraham and more in tune with our own Judaeo-Christian tradition. But the old

13 Keane, David (2008), Cartoon Violence and freedom of Expression. Human Rights Quarterly 30 845-875

hatred of Islam continues to flourish on both sides of Atlantic and people have few scruples about attacking this religion even if they know little about it."[14]

Continuing to explain the role of scholars and to keep a certain mind set of hatred for Islam she further says; "Western scholars denounced Islam as a blasphemous faith and it's Prophet as the great pretender, who had founded a violent religion of the sword in order to conquer the world. Mahomet became a bogy to the people of Europe, used by mothers to frighten disobedient children.... This inaccurate image of Islam became one of the received ideas of Europe and it continues to affect our perceptions of the Muslim World."[15]

Understanding each other is what can create a united peaceful world on grounds which do not support hatred but respect and love for all as human beings for we as human beings have experienced horrific consequences of letting hatred flourish among religions, nations and societies. Looking back in the course of history, we should understand the fact that we are living in a global village and our actions related to others are needed to be put up in accordance to the highest standards of human rights and dignity as proposed in human rights documents and recognised by the majority member states of international institutions. Regarding the matter of freedom of speech, a recognised human right in Article 19 of the UDHR and in human rights law under ICCPR is proposed. ICCPR declares it as a fundamental right and states; "everyone shall have the right to hold the opinions without interference", further it explains freedom of speech in more specific manner and says; "everyone shall have the right to freedom of expression", but the same article speaks about certain duties and responsibilities to practice freedom of speech and expression. Speaking about restrictions, Article 19 says that these are to be under law and are necessary in these two conditions; (a) for respect of the rights or reputations of others. (b) For the protection of national security or of public order, or of public health and morals. These are the highest possible morals which are learnt by the past historical mistakes of letting hatred flourish among human beings. Besides that the examples as Salman Rushdie's 'Satanic Verses', 'Burning of Quran', 'Innocence of Muslims', and 'Caricatures of The Prophet of Islam', show that we as rational human beings are ignoring past mistakes and the achieved moral standards to keep piece and harmonious global society. All such examples are not helping the cause to create a balanced

14 Armstrong, Karen. Muhammad, A western Attempt to Understand Islam. 1991. London

15 Armstrong, Karen. Muhammad, A western Attempt to Understand Islam. 1991. London

and a peaceful existence of healthy societies which is required in our globalised world. Specifically, the case of Danish cartoons is not a healthy act towards creating a peaceful harmonious global society for it was circulated around the world despite knowing that it is creating a worldwide controversy. Knowing that it is against the belief of Muslims, and a defamation of the prophet of Islam which would not make them feel easy and the opportunists of both sides would create a mess out of it; it becomes a following of footsteps of historical mistakes of creating difference among co-existing societies.[16]

Chapter 3

Legally Limiting the Freedom of Speech

3.1 Freedom of Speech; an Absolute right or not?

It is understandable at all levels of international law that freedom of speech is not last words and laws are always interpreted with all the flexibilities which are best suited. Similarly, in the case of human rights, scholars always define it along with necessary restrictions and obligations as writing on free speech Paul Sturges proposes what human rights; "Human rights are not a concept given to mankind from some external source. There is reasoning behind them and they remain open to discussion and reinterpretation".[17] We can rightly say that rights belongs to human conditions can always be reformed for the betterment of human conditions and relations. This phenomenon is explained in relation freedom of speech and expression described in international documents not being absolute right in accordance to further explanations in Article 19(3) in ICCPR as human rights law experts explains "If people may think what they like, they may not always say or right what they like. As opposed by the freedom of opinion, freedom of expression is not an absolute right. Under Article 19(3) ICCPR its exercise carries with it 'special duties and responsibilities'"[18]

16, 17Sturges, Paul (2006). Limits to freedom of expression? Considerations arising from the Danish cartoon affair.IFLA Journal 32(3) 181-188

18 Moeckli, Shah, Sivakumaran, Harris. International Human Rights Law . 2010. Oxford University Press. USA

3.2 The clash of the Rights: Freedom of Speech and Freedom of Religion

There are protections available against the protected rights if they exceed to certain extend which can be considered as exaggeration of rights to be protected against. Article10 of the European Convention of Human Rights protects the right of freedom of expression, while Article9 protects the rights related to religion and similarly in the articles 19 and 118 of the UDHR It is quite difficult to understand where does the limits of one right exceeds and where the other right begins as one can say that his freedom of religion to possess a belief is heart by using the freedom of expression by others. This situation is rightly understood by writers in the case of conflict between right to freedom of speech and the religious rights in case of both these rights as Malcom D. Evans defines how this conflict is resolved. He defines it as; "Indeed, the nature of expression at issue might remove it from the scope of protection offered by the freedom of expression altogether; just as there are forms of belief or manifestation that do not "qualify" for protection under article 9, so are there forms of expression that fall outside of the protection offered by Article 10"[19]. While defining the reasons to limit the exercise of freedom of expression Rhona Smith describes, "Rights such as freedom of expression and association are frequently only exercisable to the extent such exercise does not impinge upon the rights of others."[20]

3.3 Derogation in Case of Maintenance of International Peace and Security

Derogation is described necessary in almost every human rights instrument in times of serious threat to peace and especially international peace and security as defined by Rona Smith; "Many International and regional instruments permit derogation in times of armed conflict or other public emergencies.....which concerns to the international community in terms of the maintenance of peace and security."[21] Article18 of UDHR, Article 17 of European Convention, Article 27 of American Convention on Human Rights, and Article 4 in International Covenant on

19 Evans, Malcolm D. 2010. "From Cartoons to Crucifixes: Current Controversies Concerning the freedom of Religion and Freedom of Expression before the European Court of Human Rights" , Journal of law and Religion, pp. 345-370

20 Smith, Rona ed.4 Textbook on International Human Rights. 2010. Oxford University Press, USA

21 Smith, Rona ed.4 Textbook on International Human Rights. 2010. Oxford University Press, USA

Civil and Political Rights clearly mentions derogation as in the case of Danish Cartoons which became a problem of east and west in terms of protests and causalities.

There are few rights which are defined as non-derogable rights and religious freedom is one of its essential parts as it is supposed as a religious freedom to posses any belief and hence meant to be protected as a form of religious freedom as mentioned; "Derogation is not permitted from all aspects of the instruments: for example, there is usually no derogation from the right to life, freedom from torture, freedom from slavery, discrimination, thought, conscience and religion, or prohibition on retroactive penal legislation"[22]. In case of Danish cartoons it is belief of Muslim word that it is not permitted to present anything that manifest prophets in any physical or pictorial form as mentioned above.

3.4 Freedom of Speech and Religious Discrimination

It is a recognised phenomenon that religious differences are creating such difficulties to world peace which sometimes starts at a ignorable level as mentioned by critics; "...religious and ideological differences between major within states have been the cause of civil unrest and threat to international peace."[23] Al forms of international instruments are found condemning discrimination on the basis of religion. Articles 14 and 9 of the EU convention, 5, 6 and 8 of the Framework Convention for the Protection of National Minorities and 10, 22 of the Charter of Fundamental Rights of EU, 12 of the American Convention on Human Rights, and Article 2 of the African Charter of human and Peoples Rights hold clauses relating religious discrimination not to be exercised.

Articles 26 and 27 in ICCPR are more suited in the case of Danish Cartoons as Muslims are minority and were discriminated in their religion in comparison to others, but the 2nd Article of the "Declaration on the Elimination of all Forms of Intolerance and Discrimination Based on Religion or belief" is best suited in the situation as it mentions every level of discrimination. The similar newspaper had refused an attempt to publish cartoons of Jesus Christ and Danish government did not respond in accordance to their previous practice to combat religious intolerance and hatred in the case of Cartoons of prophet of Islam.[24]Furthermore, the editor of

22, 23Smith, Rona ed.4 Textbook on International Human Rights. 2010. Oxford University Press, USA

24 Kean, David (2008), Cartoon Violence and Freedom of Expression. Human Rights Quarterly 30 845-875

the newspaper "Jaylands Posten" Fleming Rose, stated on world media that Cartoons were only for the sake of freedom of speech and said to print cartoons on Christians and Jews in the similar manner as in case of Islam. He was not allowed to do so by his chief editor in the case of Christians and Jews.[25]

3.5 Freedom of Speech and Propaganda for Religious Hatred:

Article 20(2) of ICCPR not only prohibit but also considers it a punishable crime as it states; "Any advocacy of national, racial or religious hatred that constitute incitement to discrimination, hostility or violence shall be prohibited by law". Although, many countries have reservations on this but UNHR Committee has clearly mentioned it compatible with article 19 which preserves the right of freedom of expression and defines it as it relates to the part which bounds freedom of expression with special duties and responsibilities. The committee explains its compatibility as; "In the opinion of committee, these require prohibition are fully compatible with the right of freedom of expression as contained in article 19, the exercise of which carries with it special duties and responsibilities".[26]

In the case of Danish Cartoons, printing cartoons after clear opposition by Muslims as against their belief and defamation of their Prophet, associating him with terrorism and spreading it around the world despite knowing that Muslims are claiming it as they are deeply heart in their belief is itself a manifestation of hatred. On the other hand, opportunists used it for further damage as nationalist party representative said, Muslims want to conquer us as they did 1400 years ago which is totally against reality and clearly an attempt to spread hated in the society.

American Convention on Human Rights Article 14(5), holds restriction and punishment for the transgressor of the right to extend that he propagated such material which leads to religious hatred. Article 4 of the CERD also discourages any form of propaganda based on hatred.

---

25 Bloody Cartoons.URL http://www.youtube.com/watch?v=CipENo3kqNic&list=HL137S3J94J3 7-08-2013

26 Article 19. www.article19.org. Hate speech. URL http://www.article19.org/pages/en/hate-speech-more.html 2-08-1013

3.6 The Rights and Reputation of Others and Freedom of Speech

Human rights are universal and their universality consists of interdependency and in some cases rights prescribed in international instruments would collide with the freedoms preserved in these documents. Freedoms preserved under human rights sometimes seems halting the rights protected as in the case of freedom of expression it is observed that rights of others are violated in some cases. Under such cases it becomes a responsibility if authority to create a balance between conflicting articles of different and some times of similar documents. A decision by the human rights committee to protect right to reputation of Jews when a case "Ross V Canada" was filed can be taken as an example in which Ross made controversial public statements against Jewish faith. Although he was a teacher but his school transferred him to a non-classroom based post. The Human Rights committee considered that restriction on the author's freedom of expression, acceptable as it was for the purpose of 'protecting the "right to reputation" of persons of Jewish faith. Canada did refer to Article 20 of the international covenant in his submission to the committee.[27]

Similarly, we can consider cartoon controversy a direct defamatory act towards religion as it was against and defamation of prophet of Islam by associating him with terrorism. This provision according to law related to right to reply which is described in American Convention Article 14 (1) (2). If we read the whole article it very much seems as fulfilment of the situation created by the controversy. Article 14(1)(2) states;

1-Anyone injured by inaccurate or offensive statements or ideas disseminated to the public in general by a legally regulated medium of communication has the right to reply or make a correction using the same communication outlet, under such conditions as they may establish.

2-The correction or reply shall not in any case remit other legal liabilities that may have been incurred.

---

27 Smith, Rona ed.4 Textbook on International Human Rights. 2010. Oxford University Press, USA

Under this law we can find guidelines for both parties to act in accordance to law and if one feel injured shall behave according to law by using the same medium he can reply to the defamation.

3.7 Freedom of Speech and Universal Morals in Law

Under Article 10(2) of the European Convention relating freedom of speech is restricted for the protection of the rights of others if the right to freedom of speech and expression effects the moral obligations towards others. Cartoons of the Prophet of Islam in Denmark and throughout the world, mocking Prophet of Islam has polarised discussions and opinions on freedom of speech and expression. Lacking universal standards of public morality which is universally acceptable and not defined in legal instruments; there is enough margins for avoiding according to the parameters of the term. A very recent study shows that stereotyping Islam has grown rapidly and it is presented in a latest research completed in 2011 by centre for American progress study. They revealed that seven different organisations spent 40 million US dollars on efforts that fanned "the flames of anti-Muslim hate in America" over the last ten years.[28]

When we consider the case of Danish cartoons with the eye of moral equality and justice, we see a contrast of treatment by the media towards Islam. The role played by the newspaper is rather disappointing. As the whole issue was initiated with the decisions taken by Jayllands Posten, we have to look into his behaviour towards the phenomenon. First off the statement by Carsten Juste, the editor in chief of Jyllands Posten was itself unjustly immoral as he says:

"If I had known that the lives of Danish soldiers and civilians would be threatened, if I had known that, as my fingered hovered one centimetre above the send button for publishing the drawings, would I have hit it? No. No responsible editor in chief would have done."[29]

28 Aleaziz, Hamid. 2012, Study: Anti Islam Message Dominate Media Coverage. http://thinkprogress.org/security/2012/12/01/1268001/study-anti-muslim-group-dominate-coverage/ 2-08-2013

29 Post, Robert(2007), Religion and freedom of speech: Portraits of Muhammad, Constellation Volume 14, No1,72-90

This statement by the editor in chief of Jyllands Posten clearly out of no morals as he was making a statement after doing the damage he could have done. Firstly, his statement that he could not have done it if he knew that the lives of Danish citizens were to be lost, was itself prejudiced and biased against the humanity which does not belong to any country or nation. He should have spoken about human lose not just for humans belongs to Denmark. Secondly, He was very well aware of the situation what would have happened as number of artistes has refused to draw these cartoons knowing the consequences before his acceptance and his the call for other cartoonists to draw these cartoons.

The role played by the newspaper, Jyllands Posten was not appropriate and based on double standards towards religion and specifically Islam. The history of few years says that the Jyllands Posten have refused a demand to draw the Cartoons of Jesus Christ in past. Carens highlight this incident:

"Jyllands Posten chose not to publish some anti Christian cartoons few years previously, and at least partly justified its reactions on the grounds that it did not want to offend its readers. It is legally permissible in many places to publish racist and anti-Semitic cartoons, but major newspaper or perhaps I should say no reputable newspaper in Europe and north America would do that."[30]

It is quite clear that what was considered once immoral and below the ethics of a responsible newspaper, was not in another case. Criticising the role played by the print media, Diene's 2006 report for the Human rights Committee is the strongest attack on the publishers in an international legal document. He criticises the role played by the Danish government along with print media as he states in his report:

"These newspapers' intransigent defence of unlimited freedom of expression is out of step with international norms and seek an appropriate balance between freedom of expression and religious freedom, specifically the prohibition of incitement to religious and racial hatred."[31]

30, 31 Keane. David. (2008). Cartoon Violence and freedom of Expression. Human Rights Quarterly 30 845-875

Negative role of media in spreading hatred and contention in society is the one of the worst realities of our age. If media becomes thoroughly productive and helpfully contribute in creating bridges between differences, our world would have been better than what it is today.

3.8 Universal Human Rights and Cartoons

Freedom of speech is an essential right concerning civil and political rights professed in the universal declaration of human rights and other human rights instruments. All the instruments are based on moral rights grounded in moral reasoning derived from the society to put into laws to justify them as legal rights. Human rights' philosophers explain rights along with justified claims, duties, obligations, terms, and responsibilities. Before going towards present day terms of discussion it is helpful what the other philosophers have written for morals to be considered for the applications of freedoms.

Hobbes and Lock defined natural rights and state of nature in rather opposite way. Hobbes considers state of nature as war of everyone against others and has no duties, whereas Lock proposes moral state of nature which is only disturbed when people are biased. Both are agreed upon submitting to the authority to punish the transgressor to maintain order with obligations to respect the right of people.

Hofeld describes four ways to have rights which are claims, privileges, power and immunities. He only considered claim right as a right for it involves duties. Thomas Pogge describing rights and duties of individuals and institutions defines individuals as more vital and the main addressee of human rights as they hold moral responsibilities. Explaining "Will and Choice Theory", Kant and Hart describe on right protected to exercise freewill or self determination by the individual creates a sphere of sovereignty around each individual and he decides who can enter and on what terms. Hence, there is not any kind of moral rights explained by the philosophers of universal human rights based on unconditional freedom. Derogation can be applied in cases of dangers to peace and security. Human rights writers write about derogation accepted as universal morals by all the international and regional instruments in extreme cases when it becomes moral responsibility to the authorities to act under the laws acknowledged as moral standards;

20

"Many International and regional instruments permit derogation in times of armed conflict or other public emergencies.....which concerns to the international community in terms of the maintenance of peace and security."[32]

It is prescribed in human rights instruments that in certain situations as described, if there is a threat to international peace and security, the freedoms which become threat to peace and security can be limited to decrease to attain harmony and peace. Through the moral lens of Harm Principles by Mill and Offence Principle by Feinberg, Danish cartoons are justified to be against the moral grounds of universal human rights and contrary to the purpose of the United Nations under article 29 in the Universal Declaration of Human Rights.

We know that norms and values are the core to the law and these are norms that create laws to manifest normative requirements of a balanced and peaceful society based on equality. Human rights are dependent on understanding of the prevailing situations and the rational behaviour towards equality. Absolute justice is the only purpose of international institutions which demands impartiality in at all levels of resolving conflicts and controversies among masses. Limiting the liberties for the sake of rights is understandable to every rational mind when we all knows that how uncertain our understandings are and every other day we are progressing towards understanding of superior and better standards of human rights and justice. Human rights writers understand the value of changes in our understanding of human behaviours as it is explained;

"If people may think what they like, they may not always say or right what they like. As opposed by the freedom of opinion, freedom of expression is not an absolute right."[33]

Through the lens of John Stuart Mill's Harm Principle and Feinberg's Offence Principle the cartoons controversy can be judged if it qualifies the international norm and moral standards set by as universal moral standards.

32 Smith, Rona ed.4 Textbook on International Human Rights. 2010. Oxford University Press, USA

33 Moeckli, Shah, Sivakumaran, Harris. International Human Rights Law. 2010. Oxford University Press, USA

Chapter 4

4.1Freedom of speech under human values and norms

Most prominent philosophical theories about freedom of speech, which defines human values and norms for the existence of free speech and its limitations, are harm principle by Mill and offence principle by Feinburg. Harm principle is the first and best principle for limiting freedom of speech for it can harm. Democratic equality and paternalistic reasons have their role in limiting freedom of speech. We can reassess harm principle with the help of these criteria's. Giving higher value to free speech makes it explosive and limiting it becomes controversial.

We have to acknowledge that every society puts limits to exercise of freedom of speech as it is always in competition of values. Different scholars deny any place for unlimited speech with an argument that there had never been anything like free speech. Stanley Fish and Haworth are one of them.[34] Mill on the other end defends freedom of speech in context of liberty and authority, but one have to decide how much value should be given to freedom of speech while other ideals like privacy, security and democratic equality not less important. Fish define this phenomenon as "speech, in short, is never a value in and of itself but is always produced within the precinct of some assumed conception of the good."[35]

Arguments are presented against limiting freedom of speech as it can lead into censorship and tyranny. In reply to this argument if we do not allowing any intervention by the authorities it can lead to anarchy and the state described by Thomas Hobbes, the state of nature and life becomes solitary, poore, brutish, nasty, and short.[36] Actual exercise of legally limiting freedom of speech only makes free speech more difficult as right to free speech is different from other right for one can only be sanctioned when it has performed an action and he becomes unfree.

---

34 Van Mill, David, "Freedom of Speech", The Stanford Encyclopedia of Philosophy (Winter 2012 Edition), Edward N. Zalta (ed.),

URL: http://plato.stanford.edu/archives/win2012/entries/freedom-speech

35 Fish, Stanley. 1994. There's No Such Thing as Free Speech and it's a good thing too, Oxford University Press. USA

36 Hobbes, Thomas. 1968. Leviathan, C.B. Macpherson. Penguin Books. London

Hence we can only regulate free speech but we cannot prevent if a person is not deterred because of possible sanctions.

4.2 Mill's Harm Principle

John Stuart Mill is considered as the most famous liberal defender of free speech. He is very clear and focused about not to compromise over the right of freedom of speech at any coast as he says:

"If all mankind minus one were of one opinion, and only one person of the contrary opinion, mankind would be no more justified in silencing that one person than he, if he had the power, would be justified in silencing mankind."[37]

Furthermore, he is in favor of complete liberty when it comes to freedom of speech, he demands fullest liberty of expression is required to push over arguments to their logical limits, rather than limits of social embracement. Although he wants fullest of liberty for the dignity of person, but he does suggest the importance of the need of rules of conduct to be able to regulate the doing of members of a political community. These limits are described as harm principle and explained as;

"The only purpose, for which power can be rightfully exercised over any member of a civilized community against his will, is to prevent harm to others." [38]

Although, there are doubts about what kind of harm Mill was talking about, but it was only in case of direct harm which can invade the right of a person, and it should be very narrow for it is not easy to identify what kind of speech can harm the rights of others. Once we can distinguish what kind of speech is harmful, we would be able to limit the harmful speech. Particularly hate speech is the one must be considered if limits are to be put on any speech as most liberal democracies have put limitations on hate speech. Now if we have to justify limits on hate speech by Mills harm principle, we have to show it violates direct rights. Countries like U.K and Australia are one of the liberal societies and they have penalties in their legal systems against free speech. In U.K public order act 1986 does not need any barrier against prohibition to free

37 Mill, John. Stuart, 1978. On Liberty, Indianapolis, Hackett Publishing. USA

38 Van Mill, David, "Freedom of Speech", The Stanford Encyclopedia of Philosophy (Winter 2012 Edition), Edward N. Zalta (ed.),

URL: http://plato.stanford.edu/archives/win2012/entries/freedom-speech

speech is; "A person is guilty of an offence if he ...displays any writing, sign or other visible representation which is threatening, abusive or insulting, within the hearing or sight of a person likely to be caused harassment, alarm or distress." Australian racial discrimination act 1975 states; "It is unlawful for a person to do an act, otherwise than in private, If: (a) the act is reasonably likely in all the circumstances to offend, insult, humiliate or intimidate another person or group of people, and (b) the act is done because of race, color or national or ethnic origin". Both these laws safeguard individual's right against majority as well as of a group which is not according to Mill's harm principle. USA is totally opposite to it as there have been cases in which laws reacted for the right of the speaker against the subject. Nazi march wearing swastikas was clearly offending Jews majority residents in Skokie, Illinois where the march took place. Argument was that there was no plan of physical harm hence Jews were not harmed at all. Here main argument was harm principle as focal point becomes the harm to the speaker not to the subject of the hate. Harm principle advocates against majority tyranny as if it threatens the right of the speaker whose action was supposed against that majority for it is right of an individual or a group who can be harmed by the majority. Hence according to Mill's harm principle for the freedom of speech can only be limited if it can cause harm to the speaker and in other case it should be direct and not just psychological but physical.

4.3 Feinberg's Offence Principle

The most recent attempt to cope with the situation is Feinberg's Offence Principle. He recommends that an offence is grounded in immorality can have destructive consequences and potentially damaging. Responding to the harm principle, he suggests that it does not reach far enough and cannot shoulder all of the work necessary for a principle of free speech. He says that the harm principle sets the standards to high and that we can prohibit some forms of expression that are not appropriate and offensive. Offending someone is less serious than harming someone, Feinberg's principle reads as follows:

"it is always a good reason in support of a proposed criminal prohibition that it would probably be an effective way of preventing serious offense...to persons other than the actor, and that it is probably a necessary means to that end...The principle asserts, in effect, that the prevention of offensive conduct is properly the state's business"[39]

This kind of principle is not easy to apply for many people take offense as the result of a sensitive disposition because of unjustified prejudice. A further difficulty is that some people can be deeply offended by statements that others find mildly amusing as in the case of Danish cartoons. It is difficult to deal with such situation but offense principle operates widely in liberal democracies where citizens escape prosecution under the harm principle. Feinberg suggests that a variety of factors need to be taken into account when deciding whether freedom of expression can be justified as immoral by the offense principle. He poses four principles to assess the offence, motive of the speaker, the number of people offended, community interest, and the extent to which the offence can be avoided. These principles draw a line for morally justified claims and responsibilities.

If we look into the cartoon controversy, started from an attempt by an author wanted to write a children's book about the life of Prophet Muhammad with illustration. Not finding anyone ready to illustrate Prophet Muhammad, he appealed and at last he found chief editor of Jayllands Posten. Commenting on his intentions and not being able to find any author because they were not ready to become a part of a controversy. Joseph Carens asks: "Why would someone deliberately present information to children about another religion in a way that an author knows will be offensive to many followers of a religion? Suddenly the author's agenda doesn't appear so benign."[40] Editor of the Jayllands Posten after the protest by Muslims in Copenhagen decides to call other cartoonist to draw twelve more cartoons shows the negative motive of the speaker, not in the interest of the community at all as it was offensive to the whole 1.5 billion Muslims, and was clearly unavoidable. Looking into the motive of the newspaper Jayllands Posten knowing that it is controversial to depict religious personalities like prophets as it had refused few years back to illustrate Jesus Christ saying it is immoral to offend its readers. These deliberate acts offending a community against their will is clearly an offence and shows the motive was not a healthy one.

---

39 Van Mill, David, "Freedom of Speech", The Stanford Encyclopedia of Philosophy (Winter 2012 Edition), Edward N. Zalta (ed.),

URL: http://plato.stanford.edu/archives/win2012/entries/freedom-speech

Although under such circumstances Feinburg's offence principle suggests free speech can be limited as he says; "when fighting words are used to provoke people who are prevented by law from using a fighting response, the offense is profound enough to allow for prohibition".[40] On the other hand it is clear that crucial component of Feinburg's offence principle is that an offence can be avoided if the subject avoids offensive material and many offences as hate speech can still be allowed if it is easily avoidable. We consider, if the offence is avoidable, it should not be prohibited. In the case of Danish Cartoons, we can say if the local Muslim imams in Denmark and the general secretary of OIC had avoided the cartoons and had not spread it around the Muslim world the situation would have been different.

4.4 Democratic Values

According to Stanly Fish, to reach at a rational decision, one has to give up favoring freedom of speech in comparison to other principles and values. He suggests that values are to be given priority over free speech for we do not need hard and fast principles that could cover all speech. Our concern is a democratic society with its highly regarded values while the freedom of speech does not deal in isolation it has its affects on society. We need to compare free speech with other goods as we have to decide if it is better to value speech or privacy, security, equality or prevention of harm. In order to gain balance according to the principles of a rational society we have to understand if free speech promote or undermine our basic values. Stanley Fish explains the importance of this question in building a balanced society as he argues, "If you don't ask this question, or some version of it, but just say that speech is speech and that's it, you are mystifying—presenting as an arbitrary and unauthorized fiat—a policy that will seem whimsical or worse to those whose interests it harms or dismisses".[41]

Considering the Cartoons issue which took many lives around the world, the death threats to the cartoonists themselves, and the disorder it created in the whole world whether Muslim countries or not. We have to understand the fact that the world has become a global village and Muslims are the second religion of the West. To argue the case above, one has to dilute one's support for freedom of expression in favor of other principles, such as equal respect for all

40, 41 Keane, David. (2008), Cartoon Violence and freedom of Expression. Human Rights Quarterly 30 845-875

citizens. The task we face is obviously not to arrive at hard and fast principles that govern all speech. Instead, we have to find a workable compromise that gives due weight to a variety of values. Supporters of this view will tend to remind us that when we are discussing free speech, we are not dealing with speech in isolation. What we are doing is comparing free speech with some other good. Kavin Boyle depicts this lack of interest by a government official as:

"…this lack of official response led Danish Muslim groups to internationalize their protest."[42]

In the case of cartoons the very motive of illustrations become offensive as Joseph Carens questions why should the author needed to publish a book with controversial illustrations and when author insists desperately for his deed despite knowing it to be controversial and dangerous for community as the object is a healthy part of the community. Danish government did not respond as they refused the request by the Muslims to meet. It could have been avoided at many levels including at its initial stage when the author received lack of interest by the authors to illustrate the controversial cartoons. As a matter of fact it is not considered as moral wrong at any stage when we analyze the history of this dilemma, from its initiation up till today.

If one argue that free speech is essential for legitimacy of state which provide people develop their and exercise their talents and ability, and that was the purpose of a state not to halt right of the people to free speech. Replying to this argument, David Mill speakes to understand that a state should not capacitate a certain section of society by allowing their hate speech but should be based on justice. Philosophical principles cannot set boundaries but it is politics based on values who decides what can be said and what should not. Every situation has its value to be considered as in army where underlying value is hierarchy and authority, free speech will be more limited, but not in a university where underlying value is expression of ideas. As fish says that "regulating free speech is a defining feature of every day life.[43] Extending the state's responsibilities another view point known as paternalistic justification exists according to which state knows more than an individual what is best for him or her. Mill along with other liberals oppose it while Feinburg supports this idea as reason to limit hate speech as he says, "it can be morally legitimate for the state, by means of the criminal law, to prohibit certain types of action

---

42 Keane, David. (2008), Cartoon Violence and freedom of Expression. Human Rights Quarterly 30 845-875

43 Fish, Stanley. 1994. There's No Such Thing as Free Speech and it's a good thing too, Oxford University Press. USA

at cause neither harm nor offense to any one, on the grounds that such actions constitute or
~use evils of other kinds"[44]

we consider the cartoon controversy which became a reason of conflict and has spread in the
hole Europe. One after another country let these cartoons published and some countries
:fended it up till now. It was there democratic responsibility to uphold the democratic values
)ove all but they did not respond in these terms as Kevin Boyle describes this issue that how it
•read throughout the world:

"It should be noted that there is considerable evidence that the escalation was encouraged by
some states."[45]

Coming back to the philosophical principles of Mill and Feinburg, Mill seems more worried
)out social pressure and not ready to accept the majority tyranny and defines such situation
;, "everyone lives as under the eye of a hostile and dreaded censorship...it does not occur to
em to have any inclination except what is customary"[46] He rejects the opinion of masses as
erely average man's opinion and speaks for individuality to be pronounced more. He also
:ems acknowledging sanctions after reaching at a point where he seems uncertain of harm
inciple at social disorders as there are many acts which, being directly injurious only to the
;ents themselves, ought not to be legally interdicted, but which, if done publicly, are a violation
good manners and, coming thus within the category of offenses against others, may rightly be
·ohibited. He further explains his intentions by saying that "the liberty of an individual must be
.us far limited; he does not make himself a nuisance".[47] To him distasteful person can be held in
iption and campaign can be launched but not as a form of punishment but only if there is
ickedness in an act. If Mills want to extend his ideas of limiting to the extent of punishment he
.ust include offence principle and give up harm principle to make it a legitimate ground for
.terference with behaviour. We can experience that harm principle could not stand at difficult

Van Mill, David, "Freedom of Speech", The Stanford Encyclopedia of Philosophy (Winter 2012 Edition), Edward N. Zalta (ed.), URL:
p://plato.stanford.edu/archives/win2012/entries/freedom-speech

Keane, David. (2008), Cartoon Violence and freedom of Expression. Human Rights Quarterly 30 845-875

Mill, John. Stuart, 1978. On Liberty, Indianapolis, Hackett Publishing. USA

Keane, David. (2008), Cartoon Violence and freedom of Expression. Human Rights Quarterly 30 845-875

situation and could not defend free speech so that one cannot defend free speech only relying on principles.

Conclusion

In the case of Danish cartoons, if this exercise of freedom of expression is offensive towards Muslims as Muslims belief denounce such discrimination and for the sake religious right of Muslim such events should not let destroy world peace. Islam does not accept pictorial representation of the Prophet Muhammad (P.B.U.H.).[48] Depicting any prophet whether he belongs to any religion is not acceptable in Islam is based on a purely religious belief that it is prohibited in Quran not to defame any religious personality that belongs to other religion. A very valid and logical reason mentioned there is that they will try to defame you're religion which will hurt you. Quran says:

"And revile not those whom they call upon beside Allah, lest they, out of spit, revile Allah in their ignorance." [49]

Islam through these teachings closed any door for conflict in relation to provoke other religions or retaliate to any religious defamation. It is not seen in practice of Islam to defame any religion through immoral practice against their religious identities. No media in Islamic world ever presented cartoons of any Prophets in Judaism or Christianity ever. The conflict is most often come up on the scene between religion and secular or political world. The secular state of administration always put up their impartiality in the maters of religion which is totally against their practice. Secular forms of governments refuse all form of religious involvement in relation to positive role saying it against secular norms but they never take those against secular norms who try to defame religion.

The very purpose of religious satire is itself explained as to harm religious community as explained by Tim Benson,

".......religious satire has no such happy purpose, however......it was the direct expression of great emotional tension which was usually brought about initially by political

---

48 Sturges, Paul (2006), Limits to freedom of expression? Considerations arising from the Danish cartoon affair.IFLA Journal 32(3) 181-188

49 The Holy Quran (6: 109) translated by Moulvi Sher Ali. alislam.org, URL: http://www.alislam.org/quran/tafseer/?page=153&region=E2&CR

events but its psychological function was not to release tension by means of laughter rather the opposite."[50]

Considering the whole controversy one can easily conclude it as it resulted to be dangerous to both Muslims and Cartoonists. The harm effected cartoonists was described as: "In Saudi Arabia, two newspaper editors were sentenced to prison and to hundreds of lashes for printing a comic strip from the syndicated series "B.C." which facetiously questioned the existence of God, while in Iran, a cartoonist and his magazine editor were similarly sentenced for a soccer player adjudged to resemble the late Ayatollah Khomeini." [51]

International institutions should not let go such incident without attention as discriminating behaviors creates sense of deprivation in minorities and in case of Muslims we all know they always react violently which shows their ignorance that they destroy their own property and kill their own countrymen. Such reaction by Muslims is not supported by their teachings but it is practiced due to their Imams as in the case of Danish cartoons we experienced. There are enough laws that can be used to limit extreme conditions such as destruction of peace and security.

It is quite understandable that it is not easy to define when and how freedom of speech becomes harmful to its objects. Especially in the conflicts of liberal norms and religions for secular form of governments have drawn lines between religion and politics or government maters. This line was drawn for Christianity as west has only one religion. Just few decades back Muslims have migrated from all over the world to west and now Islam is the second religion of Europe and the west. The difference between religions can be greater than one can imagine so as in the case of Christianity and Islam, you cannot control both with same stick. Both religions are almost opposite to each other in many beliefs as in the case of sculptures and depictions of spiritual personalities. One has it as practice and other defines it totally against their religion and doing so become immoral to the extent of harmful and offensive. Dealing with Mills and Feinberg, Mill seems very strict to accept any limitations but for the extreme situations he himself turns toward offence principle and talks about sanctioning unlimited speech. Finally these are democratic values provides moral reasons for limiting freedom of expression in a

---

50 Keane, David. 2008, Cartoon Violence and freedom of Expression. Human Rights Quarterly 30 845-875

51 Dona E. Artz. 2002, The Role of Compulsion In Islamic Conversion: Jihad, Dhimma and Ridha, 8 Buffalo Hum. Rts. L. REV.15,42

liberal democratic society and Fish very clearly mentions and according to paternal justification it is state who should decide on the bases of value, when and how the freedom of speech should be limited.

Bibliography

Aleaziz, Hamid. 2012, Study: Anti Islam Message Dominate Media Coverage. URL: http://thinkprogress.org/security/2012/12/01/1268001/study-anti-muslim-group-dominate-coverage/ 2-08-2013.

Armstrong, Karen. Muhammad, A western Attempt to Understand Islam. 1991. Victor Gollancz. London.

Article 19. www.article19.org. Hate speech, URL http://www.article19.org/pages/en/hate-speech-more.html 2-08-1013.

BloodyCartoons.URL: http://www.youtube.com/watch?v=GpFNo3kqNic&list=HL1378309413 7-08-2013.

Dona E. Artz. 2002, The Role of Compulsion In Islamic Conversion: Jihad, Dhimma and Ridha, 8 Buffalo Hum. Rts. L. REV.15,42

Evans, Malcolm D. "From Cartoons to Crucifixes: Current Controversies Concerning the freedom of Religion and Freedom of Expression before the European Court of Human Rights", Journal of law and Religion, pp. 345-370. 2010.

Fish, Stanley. There's No Such Thing as Free Speech and it's a good thing too, 1994 Oxford University Press. USA

Hobbes, Thomas. 1968. Leviathan, C.B. Macpherson, Penguin Books. London

Keane, David. Cartoon Violence and freedom of Expression. Human Rights Quarterly 30. 845-875. 2008.

Mill, John. Stuart. On Liberty. Indianapolis. Hackett Publishing. 1978 USA.

Moeckli, Shah, Sivakumaran, Harris. International Human Rights Law. 2010. Oxford University Press. USA.

Post, Robert. Religion and freedom of speech: Portraits of Muhammad, Constellation Volume 14, No1, pp. 72-90. 2007.

Shelton, Dinah. Normative Hierarchy in International Law Author(s) The American Journal of International Law, Vol. 100, No. 2 pp. 29. 2006.

Smith, Rona K.M. Textbook on International Human Rights. 2010. Oxford University Press, USA

Sturges, Paul. Limits to freedom of expression? Considerations arising from the Danish Cartoon Affair, IFLA Journal 32(3) 181-188. 2006.

The Holy Quran (6: 109) translated by Moulvi Sher Ali. alislam.org, URL: http://www.alislam.org/quran/tafseer/?page=153&region=E2&CR

Weston, Anthony. A Rulebook for Arguments. 2009. Hackett Publishing Company Inc. USA

Van Mill, David, "Freedom of Speech", The Stanford Encyclopedia of Philosophy (Winter 2012 Edition), Edward N. Zalta (ed.), URL: http://plato.stanford.edu/archives/win2012/entries/freedom-speech

YOUR KNOWLEDGE HAS VALUE

- We will publish your bachelor's and master's thesis, essays and papers

- Your own eBook and book - sold worldwide in all relevant shops

- Earn money with each sale

Upload your text at www.GRIN.com and publish for free

Lightning Source UK Ltd.
Milton Keynes UK
UKOW03f0722050417
298388UK00004B/320/P